REALLY HORRIBLE FACTS

REALLY HORRIBLE BODY FACTS

Jay Hawkins

WINDMILL BOOKS™

NEW YORK

Published in 2014 by Windmill Books, LLC
303 Park Avenue South, Suite # 1280, New York, NY 10010-3657

First Edition

Editors: Samantha Noonan, Deborah Kespert, Nicola Barber, and Joe Harris
US Editor: Joshua Shadowens
Illustrations: Dynamo Ltd, Quadrum, and Steve Beaumont
Layout design: Trudi Webb

Hawkins, Jay.
Really horrible body facts / by Jay Hawkins.
  p. cm. -- (Really horrible facts)
Includes index.
ISBN 978-1-61533-743-9 (library binding) -- ISBN 978-1-61533-803-0 (pbk.) --
 ISBN 978-1-61533-804-7 (6-pack)
1. Human body--Juvenile literature. 2. Human physiology--Juvenile literature. 3. Human anatomy--
Juvenile literature. I. Hawkins, Jay. II. Title.
QP37.H39 2014
612--dc23

Printed in China
CPSIA Compliance Information: Batch #AS3102WM:
For Further Information contact Windmill Books, New York, New York at 1-866-478-0556
SL002697US

CONTENTS

Beastly Bodies 4

Outside Bits 6

Squishy Bits 8

All About Blood 10

Bones and Muscles 12

Horrible Hair, Teeth, and Nails.. 14

Toilet Tales 16

Snot, Pus, and Gunk.. 18

Sick to the Stomach 20

Nasty Noises and Stinky Smells.. 22

Ghastly Diseases 24

Worms and Worse! 26

Monstrous Medicine.. 28

Revolting Body Records.. 30

Glossary 32

Further Reading 32

Websites 32

Index 32

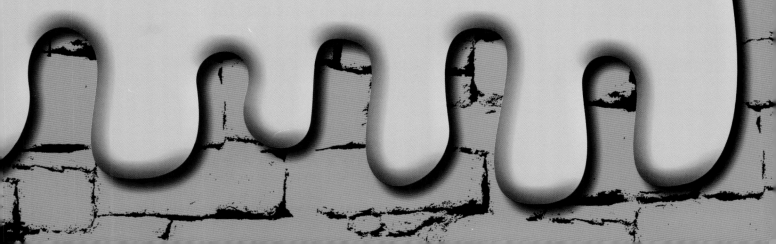

BEASTLY BODIES

Men have more nose hair than women... and it grows longer as they get older!

Sweat is made mainly of water, so it doesn't smell... until it's been around a while. Once skin bacteria have had time to slurp it up and multiply, the stink begins.

Gross!

You have mucus in your eyes! It's there to make your tear fluid spread evenly.

There are millions of things living in your mouth! Don't bother looking, though—they are microorganisms that are too small to see.

4

OUTSIDE BITS

If you kept all your loose eyelashes and lined them up, they would stretch out for 100 feet (30 m). Hopefully you'll find better ways to spend your retirement...

Nose-pickings are a mixture of dried mucus and stuff that is filtered out of the air you breathe—pollen, dust, fungus, dirt, maybe a bug or two, and even tiny particles of dust from space!

There is a fungal infection that causes the taste buds to swell and discolor, giving the tongue a black, furry appearance.

The little pink lump in the corner of your eye is what remains of an extra eyelid that our ancestors had.

If your dead skin cells didn't drop off, after three years your skin would be as thick as an elephant's!

Your belly button is the scar left from your umbilical cord. Whether it's an "innie" or an "outie" depends on the shape and size of your umbilical cord when you were born.

About 0.2 percent of the world's population has an extra finger or toe. That's 12 million people with an extra digit or two!

A single drop of blood contains 250 million blood cells.

Wow!

Mosquitoes spread malaria when they bite and pass on saliva containing parasites. The parasites then travel through the bloodstream and multiply in the liver and red blood cells.

Only a few hundred people in the world have the rarest blood type, which is H-H. They can't receive blood transfusions from any other blood group, so they sometimes need to store their own blood before an operation.

Some of your body's muscles stretch to twice their relaxed length when you exercise.

You sit on the largest muscles in your body! You have a gluteus maximus in each buttock.

After French artist Henri de Toulouse-Lautrec broke his legs in his early teens, they stopped growing. As an adult, he had a fully grown torso and child-sized legs.

You have a tailbone at the end of your spine! It is called the coccyx—meaning "cuckoo"—because it looks like a cuckoo's curved beak.

HORRIBLE HAIR, TEETH, AND NAILS

Nail fungi, bacteria, and viruses lurk in nail files... so you'd better just use your own!

They may look different, but your hair and fingernails are made from the same stuff: keratin. It's what a cow's horns and a lion's claws are made from, too!

Cola is more acidic than vinegar... and acid destroys the enamel on your teeth, so remember to brush well!

It takes six hours for a coating of plaque to form after brushing your teeth. If you don't brush it off, it eventually becomes tartar: a rock-hard substance that your dentist has to scrape off.

TOILET TALES

The average person loses 7 fluid ounces (200 ml) of water a day in their poop.

Yuck!

When diarrhea turns pale, it contains bits of the lining of your gut.

Anyone for a Japanese bird-poop facial? The special enzymes in the droppings of the Japanese Bush Warbler make it an ingredient in some anti-wrinkle treatments.

Poop smells largely because the microbes in your gut produce two stinky chemicals as they work to break down your food—indole and skatole.

About a third of your poop is not old food, but bacteria that help you to digest food, and bits of the lining of the inside of your gut.

The toilet paper used in the United States in one day would go around the world nine times.

If you ever want to classify what you leave behind in the toilet, you should take a look at the Bristol Stool Chart. The seven types of stool listed range from "separate hard lumps, like nuts" (Type 1) to "entirely liquid" (Type 7).

Gross!

SNOT, PUS, AND GUNK

A bad gum infection called gingivitis can lead to pus-filled mouth sores, purple gums, and the stinkiest of stinky breath.

Your nose is busy making mucus all day long, but you swallow most of it—about one cupful. Gross!

People in ancient India inoculated themselves against smallpox by rubbing pus from an infected person into a scratch on their bodies.

If your vomit looks like what you've just eaten, that's exactly what it is. If it's soupy, then it's because it's been in your stomach for a while.

The longest recorded distance for projectile vomiting is 27 feet (8 m)!

If you throw up and your vomit is greenish, it contains bile from your intestine, not just your stomach. The bile and stomach acid make vomit taste awful.

Vomit is a yucky cocktail of half-digested food, stomach mucus, saliva, and gastric acids.

20

NASTY NOISES AND STINKY SMELLS

French doctor Frédéric Saldmann insists that people should burp, fart, and sweat freely to reduce the risk of cancer.

Gross!

The 250,000 sweat glands in your feet make them one of the sweatiest parts of the body. Adults produce two whole cups of that stinky foot juice every week!

Does your tummy ever rumble or growl? The official name for it is borborygmus and it's the sound of muscles contracting in your digestive system.

When a dead body is decomposing (rotting), the bacteria inside it produce gases. When the gas is released from the body, it sounds like a fart!

When you cough, air rushes through your windpipe at 60 miles per hour (100 km/h).

If you eat asparagus, your urine will smell of rotten cabbages! The stink comes from a gas called methanethiol, which is produced when you digest the vegetable.

Yuck!

What you hear when you fart is the vibration of your sphincter muscles as air passes through them. The sort of sound you get depends on how fast the air is going.

GHASTLY DISEASES

The most deadly animal in the world is the mosquito. They spread viruses and parasites that kill millions of people every year.

Both humans and cats can carry a disease called toxoplasmosis. Some scientists think that the disease makes humans like cats more, so that they pass it on!

Rat fleas spread the deadly disease bubonic plague. Although it's rare these days, the illness killed around one third of the population of 14th-century Europe, when it was known as the "Black Death."

24

One of the most common diseases found in water is cryptosporidiosis. Microscopic parasites swallowed in water hatch inside the intestine and cause severe diarrhea.

A tiny amount of rat pee can make you very sick. Weil's disease comes from rats' urine and is caught from infected water.

Indonesian fisherman Dede Koswara suffers from a rare genetic disorder. His body reacted to a wart virus by covering his skin with huge growths that look like tree bark.

The common cold can be caused by 200 different viruses.

WORMS AND WORSE!

You don't have to ingest hookworms to catch them—they can bore through the skin on your feet!

You have at least a million dust mites crawling around your mattress and pillow, gobbling up all your old skin cells.

In severe cases of worms, a large group can clump together in a ball and cause a blockage in the intestines or bowel.

The female chigoe flea lays her eggs by burrowing into human skin head-first, leaving her back end sticking out. Over two weeks, she feeds on blood and lays about 100 eggs, before dying and falling out.

Demodex mites are tiny parasites that live in eyebrows and eyelashes. They're very common, especially in older people. Under a microscope, they look like worms with stubby legs.

The best reason to check for head lice is the saying that "what goes in must come out." Yep, if they're feeding on your blood, they're pooping in your hair!

A broad tapeworm can grow in the intestine for decades, reaching a length of 33 feet (10 m). Worst of all, you may not even know you have one...

MONSTROUS MEDICINE

Robert Liston was the fastest surgeon in 19th-century Scotland. He could carry out an amputation in just 30 seconds.

Gross!

One medieval treatment for a skin infection was to rub cow dung on it.

Early X-rays caused nasty side effects such as skin burns, swelling, and hair loss.

Surgeons occasionally leave things behind during operations. Things that have been sewn inside patients include clamps, surgical sponges, scalpels, scissors, forceps, and doctors. Okay, only kidding about the last one!

REVOLTING BODY RECORDS

Sometimes, small crystals made of waste products are formed in the kidneys. These are called kidney stones. The most stones ever removed from one kidney was 728!

The deadliest natural toxin comes from bad food. A toxin called clostridium botulinum is more poisonous than arsenic or snake venom and causes the deadly paralyzing illness botulism.

British performer Scott Bell has super-tough feet—he has walked more than 300 feet (90 m) over burning hot embers.

30

The largest object ever removed from a skull was an 18-inch (46 cm) long drill bit. Californian construction worker Ron Hunt fell off a ladder and landed face first onto it. He lost an eye but escaped brain damage.

Anthony Victor of India has the longest ear hair in the world, measuring 7.1 inches (18.1 cm).

The loudest snore ever recorded was 93 decibels— that's louder than a car engine!

How many people can you fit into a compact car? The record is 22—but they didn't look too comfortable.

GLOSSARY

bacteria (bak-TIR-ee-uh) Tiny one-celled organisms, some of which cause disease.

enzyme (EN-zym) Something that helps a chemical reaction to happen inside a cell.

inoculate (ih-NAH-kyoo-layt) To give someone a mild form of an illness in order to protect them from a more serious form.

parasite (PER-uh-syt) An organism that lives and feeds off another organism.

virus (VY-rus) An organism that lives and multiplies inside the cells of a host.

FURTHER READING

Bredeson, Carmen. *Weird But True Human Body Facts.* Berkeley Heights, NJ: Enslow Elementary, 2011.

Dorling Kindersley. *First Human Body Encyclopedia.* New York: DK Publishing, 2012.

Toufexis, George. *The Outrageous Human Body Activity Book.* Mineola, NY: Dover Publications, 2013.

WEBSITES

For web resources related to the subject of this book, go to: www.windmillbooks.com/weblinks and select this book's title.

INDEX

blood 10, 11, 19, 26

bones 12, 13, 19

eyes 4, 6, 7, 24, 27, 31

feet 22, 26, 30

hair 4, 14, 15, 27, 28, 31

infections 5, 10, 18, 24, 25, 28

intestines 5 25, 26, 27

kidneys 8, 30

mucus 4, 6, 18, 19, 20

muscles 12, 13

nails 14, 15

skin 4, 5, 7, 16, 25, 26, 28

stomach 20, 21, 22

teeth 14, 15, 29